NATURE CLOSE-UP

Mantids

and Their Relatives

TEXT BY ELAINE PASCOE

PHOTOGRAPHS BY DWIGHT KUHN

BLACKBIRCH PRESS
An imprint of Thomson Gale, a part of The Thomson Corporation

THOMSON

GALE

Detroit • New York • San Francisco • San Diego • New Haven, Conn. • Waterville, Maine • London • Munich

LIBRARY OF CONGRESS CATALOGING-IN-PUBLICATION DATA

Pascoe, Elaine.
  Mantids / by Elaine Pascoe ; photographs by Dwight Kuhn.
      p. cm. — (Nature close-up)
  Includes index.
  ISBN 1-4103-0307-1 (alk. paper)
  1. Mantodea—Juvenile literature. I. Kuhn, Dwight. II. Title III. Series: Pascoe, Elaine.
Nature close-up.

  QL505.83.P37 2004
  595.7'27—dc22   2004007270

Printed in China
10 9 8 7 6 5 4 3 2 1

Contents

1

Praying or Preying?

A mantid sits perfectly still on a branch. Its front legs are folded as if it were silently praying. But the mantid isn't praying—it's hunting. When another insect comes near, the mantid strikes. In a flash, it grabs its prey with its front legs. Sharp spines on the legs hold the victim tight, and the mantid begins to eat.

The mantid is a fierce hunter. It strikes with its forelegs to catch its prey.

Mantids are extraordinary insects. Many people call these insects "praying mantises" for the way they hold their forelegs when they are waiting for prey. With their unusual appearance and odd ways, mantids are fascinating to watch.

The mantids' closest relatives in the insect world are cockroaches. You probably know cockroaches as household pests. But only a few types of roaches invade people's homes. Most types never bother people— and some are even kept as pets.

A young mantid waits on a flower for insect prey to come near.

6

Hidden Hunters

There are about 1,800 different kinds, or species, of mantids worldwide. Most live in tropical places, but about 20 kinds are found in North America. Mantids range in size from $5/8$ inch (1.6 cm) to more than 6 inches (15 cm) long as adults. Two kinds that are native to the United States, the Carolina mantid and the California mantid, are about 2 inches (5 cm) long. Chinese mantids, also found in the United States, are often twice as long.

Most mantids are green, yellowish, or brown. They look like leaves or twigs, so they blend in well with bushes and other plants. This **camouflage** helps hide them from their prey. Some tropical mantids even mimic the colors of the flowers where they lie in wait for prey.

This mantid looks just like a leaf of the plant on which it rests.

7

Like all insects, mantids have an outer shell, or **exoskeleton**, instead of a bony skeleton. They have six legs and three body regions: head, **thorax**, and abdomen. Males are usually a bit smaller than females, and their abdomens are thinner.

The thorax is where the insect's legs and wings are attached. The mantid's oversized front legs are especially designed to catch prey. From their folded, "praying" position, the legs can strike out faster than the eye can see. Long sharp spines on the insides of these legs hold on to the prey. The legs also have a defensive role. When a mantid is threatened, it may rear up and raise its forelegs to scare off its attacker.

When a mantid is threatened, it rears up to defend itself.

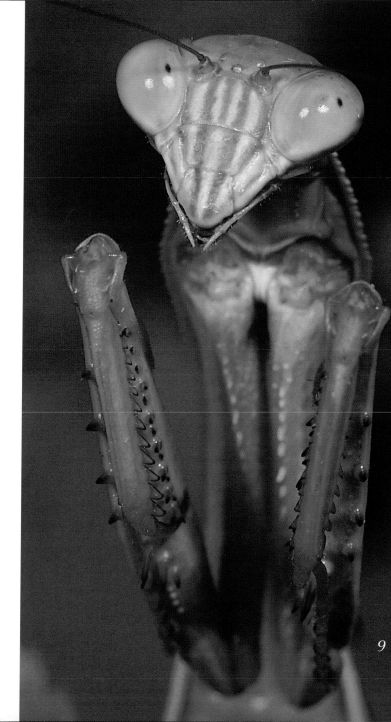

The forward part of the mantid's thorax is narrow, making a sort of neck. The insect's head is shaped like a triangle. A mantid can move its head much more freely than most insects can. This lets it look all around for prey without moving its body. The mantid has two large **compound eyes** that see colors and images. It also has three smaller eyes that probably see only light and dark. It feels and smells with pair of long, thin antennae.

By twisting its head, the mantid can see in all directions with its huge compound eyes.

9

Most of the time, the mantid waits for prey to come near.
But sometimes it stalks its prey, creeping slowly along a branch.
Mantids catch and eat anything they can, including other mantids.
They are among the few insect predators that are fast enough to
catch mosquitoes and flies. Large mantids can catch crickets,
grasshoppers, butterflies, and moths. There are even reports of
large mantids catching hummingbirds!

For such a fierce predator, the mantid has a fairly small mouth.
It bites its prey at the neck, to stop its struggling. Then it eats the
prey like an ice cream cone, starting at the neck and nibbling down
toward the tail. After eating, a mantid often grooms itself. It uses
its mouth to clean its front legs with catlike motions.

*Right: A mantid holds a beetle with its forelegs and eats
it from the neck down.*

Inset: After eating, a mantid cleans its legs with its mouth.

11

Mantid Life Cycle

Mating is risky for mantid males. The male leaps onto the female's back. She may turn around, grasp him, and start to eat him as they mate. But just as often, he jumps away and survives. Strangely, the male can finish mating even if the female bites his head off.

The female lays her eggs in the fall. Depending on the species, one female may lay from 30 to 300 eggs. She places a mass of eggs on a branch or tree trunk or, sometimes, the side of a building. The mass is covered with a frothy liquid that hardens to form a protective case.

Left: Mantids mating. The female has bitten off the male's head, but mating continues.

Right: The female lays a mass of eggs on a tree branch.

13

Adult mantids usually die in the fall, not long after the eggs are laid. In spring, young mantids, called **nymphs**, hatch and break out of the case. They look like tiny adults, but they have no wings. The nymphs begin to catch and eat prey right away. They prey on aphids and other small insects. If they don't see other prey, they go after each other.

Mantid young, called nymphs, break out of the egg case.

The nymphs feed and grow through spring and into summer. As it grows, a nymph must **molt**, or shed its skin. The nymph finds a stem or twig and dangles from it on a silken thread. Then it splits open its exoskeleton and wriggles free. Right after molting, the nymph is soft and milky white. But its new, larger exoskeleton quickly hardens and darkens.

A mantid nymph molts, shedding its old skin and stepping out in a new, bigger skin.

15

A mantid nymph molts six or more times. With each molt, wing buds on the insect's back get bigger. Finally it molts one last time and steps out with complete wings. It has become an adult.

Mantids are not strong fliers, but adult males often fly around at night. They can sometimes be seen around porch lights in late summer. They are a favorite prey of bats, which hunt after sunset. Some mantids have a structure on the thorax that lets them hear the sound waves that bats send out as they fly.

After its final molt, the mantid has wings. It is an adult.

MANTID LORE

The name *mantis* comes from the Greek word for prophet or soothsayer. The ancient Greeks may have thought this insect looked like a prophet trying to gaze into the future.

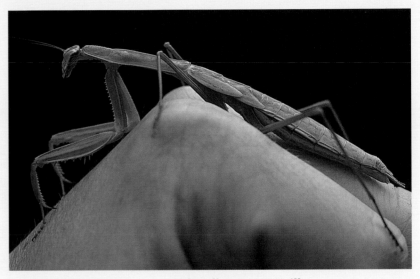

If you hold still when a mantid walks on you, will you have good luck?

Mantids have fascinated people since ancient times. They were thought to be good luck in many African cultures. In the African country of Senegal, an old superstition says that you should hold still if a mantid walks on you. If you don't chase it away, you will have good fortune.

There are lots of other beliefs about mantids. One holds that mantids can guide you home if you are lost. Just note which way a mantid is pointing as it rests on a branch, and head in that direction. Another belief is that mantids always face toward the Muslim holy city of Mecca, as Muslims do in prayer. There's no truth to these beliefs, however.

People are still fascinated by mantids. In the martial arts, the stealth and speed of these insects has inspired a kung-fu style called mantis. And two U.S. states have adopted mantids as their official state insects. They are Connecticut (European praying mantis) and South Carolina (Carolina mantis).

A cockroach is an unwelcome lunch guest.

Cockroaches

There are nearly 4,000 species of cockroaches worldwide. Most of them live in tropical regions. Of the 55 types found in the United States, no more than 5 or 6 are pests. The rest live in the wild and don't bother people.

Many types of cockroaches live in the leaf litter on the forest floor. Some live in caves. Some burrow in the ground, and some bore into wood. In Australia, there are giant burrowing cockroaches, called rhinoceros cockroaches, that grow up to 3 inches (8 cm) long. Their tunnels run as deep as 3 feet (almost 1 m) underground. The insects come out at night to collect leaf litter, which they take down to their burrows to eat.

Rhinoceros roaches have no wings. But in South America, some flying cockroaches are up to 4 inches (10 cm) long, with a **wingspan** of more than 7 inches (18 cm).

The smallest cockroaches live inside the nests of North American leaf-cutter ants. These ants bite off bits of leaves and carry them back to their nests. A type of fungus grows on the leaf cuttings and provides food for the ants. It also provides food for the tiny cockroaches, which are less than 1/16 inch (1.5 mm) long.

Cockroaches are among the most ancient types of insects. They were around long before the dinosaurs. Scientists have found **fossils** of giant flying cockroaches that lived 300 million years ago. Some scientists think ancient cockroaches may even have been the first animals to fly.

Cockroaches haven't changed much in their millions of years on earth. The cockroaches of today are not very different from their ancient fossil ancestors. These insects are mostly flat and oval in shape. Most types are drab brown. But some tropical cockroaches have bright colors and patterns.

This cockroach looks much like its ancient ancestors, which lived hundreds of millions of years ago.

A cockroach checks out food with its sensitive antennae. These insects eat almost anything.

Cockroaches have sensitive antennae that help them find food and water. Unlike mantids, they are not **predators**. Most are **scavengers**. They eat just about anything they find, as long as it is of plant or animal origin. In homes, roaches will even eat the glue in book bindings. In the wild, they are part of the natural cleanup crew that helps break down dead plant and animal material. They are also food for birds, lizards, and other small animals. Thus they have an important role to play in the natural world.

Many cockroaches are **nocturnal**, or active at night, and run from light. If you have ever tried to swat a cockroach, you know that these insects can be hard to catch. A cockroach can sense tiny movements in the air through its cerci, sensory structures at the rear of its abdomen. This allows it to scoot away from danger at the last minute. Most cockroaches can run fast, and the smaller kinds can squeeze into tiny cracks to hide. They have a slick outer covering, or cuticle, that helps them slide through tight spaces.

Like mantids, female cockroaches cover their eggs in a foamy egg case. The females of many types put the egg case in a protected place and leave it. But female German cockroaches carry their egg cases around for about three weeks until the eggs are ready to hatch. Like mantid nymphs, young cockroaches molt several times before they become adults.

21

ROACH RECORDS

Fastest — Roaches hold the insect land speed record. Certain large tropical cockroaches can scuttle along at more than 3 miles (4.8 km) per hour. This may not sound fast, but it works out to about 50 body lengths per second. That would be like a horse galloping 200 miles (322 km) an hour.

Toughest — A cockroach can live a week without its head. Like most insects, it has a very simple nervous system. Instead of a complicated brain like yours, it has a series of nerve centers strung along the underside of its body. It can do many things, including walking, without its head. But it can't eat or drink, so eventually it dies.

Most productive — The German cockroach breeds year-round. A female German cockroach can produce 300 offspring in her lifetime, which is about 6 months. If half the offspring are females, and each of those females produces 300 nymphs, there will be 45,000 roaches within a year.

Roaches are among the most successful creatures on earth.

A grasshopper rests on a flower. Unlike mantids, grasshoppers are plant eaters.

Some scientists place cockroaches and mantids in a large group of insects that includes crickets, grasshoppers, and walking sticks. These insects have lots in common. But there are also lots of differences among them, so other scientists put them in different insect groups. Walking sticks look like little twigs. Crickets and grasshoppers "sing" by rubbing body parts—wings or legs—together. Like cockroaches, crickets eat just about anything. Grasshoppers and walking sticks mostly eat plants.

Because they are such good hunters, mantids can help control insect pests in gardens.

Mantids, Cockroaches, and People

Mantids are **beneficial** insects. They do not bite people, damage houses, invade food supplies, or spread disease. Gardeners love them because they catch and kill many insects that harm plants. However, they also feed on other beneficial insects— including each other.

Two kinds of mantids found in the United States today are not native to North America. They were first imported about 75 years ago to help control insect pests in gardens. The European mantid is pale green and about 3 inches (more than 7 cm) long. The Chinese mantid is green and light brown and grows up to 5 inches (more than 12 cm) long. Both insects can now be found in the wild.

People are not so fond of the mantids' close relatives, the cockroaches. As household pests, cockroaches can spread disease. Some people have severe allergic reactions to their droppings.

The most widespread cockroach pest in the United States is the German cockroach. It is light brown and about 1/2 inch (15 mm) long. People brought the German cockroach to North America—although they didn't mean to. It's one of several kinds of cockroaches that have spread around the world by hiding in the cargo of ships.

It's important to remember that most kinds of cockroaches are not pests. Some of these insects are even kept as pets. The Madagascar hissing cockroach is sometimes sold in pet shops. Most cockroaches are silent, but this insect hisses loudly. It's big, moves slowly, and can't fly —so it's not likely to escape.

Some types of cockroaches are household pests. But many other kinds don't bother people.

25

Collecting and Caring for Mantids

To find mantids in the wild, look in gardens and fields in summer and early fall. You will have to look closely, because mantids can be hard to spot in their camouflage colors. Check flowering plants and other plants that attract insects. You may find a mantid waiting to catch an insect on these plants. After dark in late August and September, adult mantids may fly to outdoor lights.

Summer and fall are good times to find mantids outdoors.

In winter and early spring, you may find mantid egg cases on the branches of shrubs or other plants. You can also buy egg cases from many places, including the mail order suppliers listed at the end of this book. If you put the cases outside in your yard, mantid nymphs will hatch from the eggs in spring. They may help control pests in your garden.

You can also hatch the nymphs and raise them indoors. Mantids are not difficult to raise. But they require a lot of work and attention because they need live insect prey. This chapter will tell you how to care for them. After you are done watching them, release them into your garden or a park or wild area.

Mantids lay their eggs in the fall. Look for egg cases on branches in early spring.

To collect an egg case, clip the twig or branch that it's on.

Egg Cases

To collect an egg case that you've found, carefully cut the twig that it's attached to. The twig will give the nymphs something to crawl onto when they hatch. Egg cases that you buy usually come with twigs attached. If not, you may be able to slide a twig into a groove on the egg case. (The groove was formed by the twig on which the egg case was originally laid.) Or you can glue a twig to the back (flattened) side of the case.

The eggs need two to four weeks of warm temperatures, 75°F (24°C) or more, to hatch. If you bring them indoors in winter, they may hatch before other insects are around to serve as their food. Leave the egg cases outside until you know that you will be able to provide the young insects with food or release them with a good chance of survival.

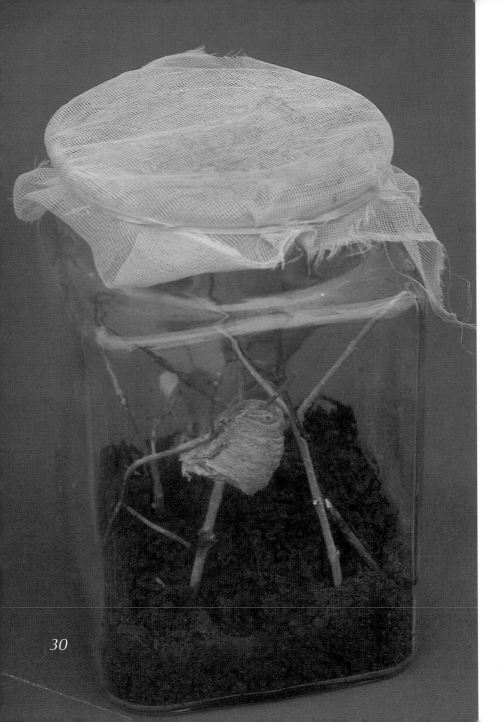

A Mantid Home

Set up a container for your mantids before they hatch. Put some moist soil in the bottom. You can add growing plants if you want. Plants and soil will help provide moisture that the young insects need.

Prop the twig with the egg case against the side of the container so that the wider end of the egg case points down. If there are not many plants in the container, add extra sticks and twigs to give the nymphs places to climb when they hatch. Cover the top of the container with cheesecloth or fine screening. Put it in a warm place.

A container for a mantid egg case has moist soil, twigs, and a live plant.

Hatching

As many as 100 young mantids may hatch from an egg case. You can release some of the nymphs in your garden and keep others, so you can watch them grow. It may be difficult to provide enough insects to feed many nymphs, so you may want to only keep a few.

The mantids need food soon after hatching, or they will begin to eat each other. You can prevent this by putting the insects into individual containers. Any small container, such as a baby-food jar, will do. Give each mantid a small twig or leaf to climb on. Cover the container with cheesecloth and a rubber band.

It's possible to keep several mantises in a single container. But you'll need to provide a steady supply of live insects for them to eat, so they don't go after each other.

Dozens of nymphs hatch from an egg case. They are all hungry.

31

Feeding Mantids

In warm weather you can feed your mantids aphids and other small insects that you find outdoors. Look for these insects on garden plants. You can also buy fruit flies year-round from most biological supply houses and stores that sell live food for fish and reptiles. These suppliers sell wingless fruit flies that won't fly away when you put them in the mantis container.

The flies arrive in little bottles, or vials. To feed the mantids, tap the vial on a table so most of the flies drop to the bottom. Then quickly open the top and drop a few flies into your mantid container. A few flies per mantid per day are enough at first. Cover the container quickly before flies or mantids get out. If you find that the flies are too fast to handle, chill the flies in their container in the freezer for just a minute or two. The cold temperature will slow them down.

Mantids need moisture, too. Supply it by spraying a fine mist of water on the inside walls of their container once a day. Keep the mantid container in a warm place, but not in direct sunlight.

Wingless fruit flies are a good food for young mantis nymphs.

A mantis nymph eats a fruit fly. Larger mantids can eat larger insects, such as crickets.

As the mantids grow, they will need more flies or aphids. Larger mantids can eat larger insects. Small crickets, which you can buy at most pet shops, work well.

You can keep a supply of live crickets on hand by setting up a cricket home. Use an aquarium or similar container. Put a layer of sand in the bottom. Add some paper towels or an egg carton to give the crickets places to hide.

Provide water for the crickets in a small container or jar lid. Put a cotton ball in the water container, so the crickets will be able to get to the moisture without falling in and drowning. Feed them cornmeal, oatmeal, bits of raw potato, and lettuce leaves.

Investigating Mantids

In this section, you'll find projects and activities that will help you learn more about mantids. Some of the projects can be done with mantid eggs that you find outside or order through the mail, and others can be done with mantid nymphs or adults. Have fun with these activities. When you're done, return the insects to the place where you found them, or release them in a park or garden.

Do Mantid Eggs Hatch Sooner in Sunlight or Shade?

Mantid eggs are protected by their case through the winter. The nymphs hatch in spring. What role does sunlight play in their hatching? Decide what you think, and then do this activity to find out. Start the activity in early spring, several weeks before mantids usually hatch. You can use egg cases that you buy or find.

What to Do:

1. If your egg cases are not attached to twigs, look for a groove on the back (flatter) side of the case. You may be able to slide a twig into the groove. If not, glue a stick or twig to the back of the case.

What You Need:
- 2 mantid egg cases
- Twist ties, tape, or clothespins

2. Attach one egg case to a tree branch or another place outside where it will get plenty of sun. Tie, tape, or clothespin the twig with the mantis case to the branch. Make sure the fatter part of the egg case points down.

3. Attach the second egg case in the same way, but in a place where it will be in shade. A tree or shrub on the north side of a building may work well.

4. Check both cases every day to see if the mantids have hatched. They normally hatch in mid- to late morning.

Results: Which egg case hatches first, or do both hatch at about the same time?

Conclusion: What do your results tell you about the role of sunlight in hatching? If sunlight made a difference, why do you think it did?

How Much Can a Mantid Nymph Eat in a Day?

Mantid nymphs always seem to be hungry. But just how many insects can one little nymph eat? Make your best guess, based on what you know about these insects. Then do this activity to see if you are right.

What to Do:

1. Put the twig or leaf in the container, to make a perch for the mantis. Then add the mantis nymph and cover the container with mesh, secured with a rubber band. Follow the care instructions in chapter. Keep the container out of direct sunlight and mist with water daily.

37

2. Add insect prey, as described in chapter 2. If the nymph is very small, use fruit flies bought from suppliers or aphids collected from plants. Larger mantids can eat tiny crickets bought at pet stores. Cover the container quickly after you add the insects.

3. Count the live insects that you add to the jar. There should be about 12. Don't include dead flies or crickets in the count.

4. After 24 hours, count again.

Results: How many insects are left after 24 hours? How many did the mantid eat? Repeat the experiment. Do you get the same results?

Conclusion: What do your results tell you about what mantids need to survive? What factors could affect a mantid's appetite?

You can also do this experiment with an adult mantid, if you find one. Feed it crickets, grasshoppers, or flies.

Will a Mantid Nymph Molt Sooner If It Is Fed More?

Most mantid nymphs molt six to nine times before they are adults. Will a ready supply of food speed up molting? Decide what you think, and then do this experiment to find out.

What to Do:

1. Place each nymph in a jar. Give each one a twig or a leaf as a perch, and cover the jar with mesh and a rubber band.

What You Need:

- 2 newly hatched mantid nymphs, both the same size
- Fruit flies or aphids
- 2 small jars or similar containers
- Twigs or leaves
- Mesh and rubber band

2. Add live fruit flies or aphids to the jars every day. Feed one nymph one fly or aphid each day, and give the other nymph 12 flies each day.

3. Keep the jars in the same place, so they are at the same temperature. Follow the care instructions in chapter 2. Keep the containers out of direct sunlight and mist with water daily.

4. Watch to see when the nymphs molt.

Results: Did one nymph molt first? Repeat the experiment with several other mantids to check your results.

Conclusion: How does food supply affect the way mantid nymphs grow?

What Does a Mantid Prefer —Live or Dead Insects?

In the wild, mantids hunt live prey. But would a mantid just as soon dine on dead insects? Based on what you have read about mantids, decide what you think. Then do this experiment. You can use adult mantids or nymphs.

What You Need:

- 2 mantids
- 2 small containers
- Twigs and leaves
- Mesh and rubber bands
- Live and dead insects for food

What to Do:

1. Set up a container for each mantid. Give each a twig or a leaf as a perch. After you put the mantids in, cover the containers with mesh and a rubber band. Follow the care instructions in chapter 2. Keep the containers out of direct sunlight and mist with water daily.

2. Add a dead insect to one container and a live insect to the other. For small nymphs, use fruit flies or aphids. For larger nymphs, use small crickets. For adults, use crickets, grasshoppers, or beetles.

41

Results: Check the containers to see what the mantids eat. Repeat the experiment—give a dead insect to the mantid that had the live insect before, and give the other mantid a dead insect. (Be sure to feed a mantid its preferred food if it hasn't eaten in a few days.)

Conclusion: What do your results tell you about the way mantids feed? Repeat the experiment with other mantids, or with different types of insect prey. Are your results the same?

More Activities with Mantids

1. Take a close look at a mantid. Use a hand lens to look at its compound eyes, mouthparts, and powerful forelegs.
2. Watch a mantid move. Place the insect on a branch. Does it try to run or hide? Which way does it go?
3. Watch a mantid hunt. If no prey insects are near, tempt the mantid with a raisin attached to a piece of thread. Jiggle the raisin in the air, so it looks like a fly. What does the mantid do? What sense does it use to track its prey? How can you tell?
4. Watch mantid nymphs hatch. Find an egg case, or buy one and put it in your garden in spring. Check every day to see if the nymphs have hatched. This usually happens in mid- to late morning. What do the tiny insects do when they come out? How many come out of the egg case?

Results and Conclusions

Here are some possible results and conclusions for the activities on pages 34 to 42. Many factors may affect the results of these activities. If your results differ, try to think of reasons why. Repeat the activity with different conditions, and see if your results change.

Do mantid eggs hatch sooner in sunlight or in shade?
Expect the eggs in sunlight to hatch sooner. The sun provides warmth, which speeds up the growth of insects. Cold normally slows down the growing process.

How much can a mantid nymph eat in a day?
The number of insects eaten will vary depending on when the mantid last ate, how big it is, how big the prey is, and other factors. In our experiment small nymphs ate about eight fruit flies in 24 hours.

Will a mantid nymph molt sooner if it is fed more?
One fly a day should be enough to keep a mantid nymph healthy. In general, mantises fed more do grow faster. But other factors may also affect growth.

What does a mantid prefer—live or dead insects?
Mantids only go for live, moving prey. They don't eat insects that are already dead.

Some Words About Mantids

beneficial Helpful.

camouflage Coloring and patterns that help living things blend in with their surroundings.

compound eyes Eyes that have many lenses, or facets.

exoskeleton The hard outer skin of an insect. It takes the place of an internal skeleton.

fossils Preserved remains of ancient living things.

molt To shed the skin.

nocturnal Active at night

nymph An immature form of certain insects. Nymphs often look like adults without wings.

predators Animals that kill and eat other animals.

scavengers Animals that eat what they find, usually dead material.

thorax The center section of an insect's body. Usually the legs and wings are attached here.

wingspan The measurement from the tip of one outstretched wing to the other.

45

Sources for Mantids

You can buy mantid egg cases from sources such as these.

Carolina Biological Supply Company
2700 York Road
Burlington, NC 27215
(800) 334-5551
www.carosci.com

Connecticut Valley Biological Supply
82 Valley Road, P.O. Box 326
Southampton, MA 01073
(800) 628-7748
www.ctvalleybio.com

Science Kit and Boreal Laboratories
777 E Park Drive, P.O. Box 5003
Tonawanda, NY 14150
(800) 828-7777
www.sciencekit.com

For More Information

Books

Larry Dane Brimner, *Praying Mantises*. Danbury, CT: Childrens Press, 1999.

David George Gordon, *The Compleat Cockroach: A Comprehensive Guide to the Most Despised (and Least Understood) Creature on Earth*. Berkeley, CA: Ten Speed Press, 1996.

Jinny and Jimmy Johnson, *Simon & Schuster Children's Guide to Insects and Spiders*. New York, NY: Simon & Schuster, 1997.

Sally Kneidel, *Pet Bugs: A Kid's Guide to Catching and Keeping Touchable Insects*. Hoboken, NJ: John Wiley & Sons, 1994.

Elizabeth Scholl, *Praying Mantis*. San Diego, CA: Kidhaven Press, 2004.

Christina Wilsdon, *Insects (National Audubon Society First Field Guides)*. New York, NY: Scholastic, 1998.

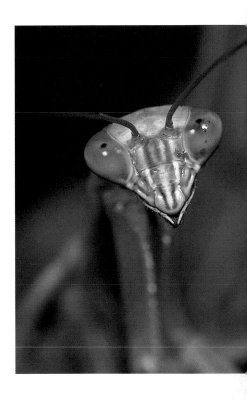

Web Sites

Insecta Inspecta
www.insecta-inspecta.com
Information about mantids and other insects.

Yucky Roach World
yucky.kids.discovery.com/roaches
Amazing cockroach facts and more.

Index